# Table of Content

Table of Content ........................................................ 1

Chapter 1: Introduction ............................................ 4

- Brief overview of North Dakota and its attractions ...... 5

- Why North Dakota is a unique travel destination ........ 8

Chapter 2: History of North Dakota .......................... 10

- Overview of the state's history and how it has shaped its current attractions ............................................. 11

Chapter 3: Natural Attractions ................................. 13

- Exploring the beauty of North Dakota's national and state parks ............................................................. 14

- Outdoor activities such as hiking, fishing, and wildlife spotting ................................................................. 16

Chapter 4: Cultural Attractions ............................... 18

- Discovering North Dakota's rich Native American heritage ................................................................. 19

- Visiting museums, art galleries, and historical sites . 22

Chapter 5: Adventure Tourism ................................. 24

- Thrilling experiences such as zip-lining, rock climbing, and water sports .................................................... 25

- Exploring North Dakota's unique landscapes through adventure tours ........................................................ 28

Chapter 6: Culinary Experiences ............................... 30

- Local cuisine and dining options in North Dakota .... 32

- Farmers markets, food festivals, and wineries to visit ........................................................................... 35

Chapter 7: Small Town Charm ................................... 37

- Exploring the quaint towns and communities of North Dakota ................................................................... 38

- Meeting locals and experiencing small town hospitality ........................................................................... 41

Chapter 8: Family-Friendly Attractions ...................... 43

- Fun activities for the whole family in North Dakota ... 44

- Zoos, amusement parks, and family-friendly museums ........................................................................... 47

Chapter 9: Historic Sites ............................................ 49

- Visiting historical landmarks and monuments in North Dakota ................................................................... 50

- Learning about the state's role in U.S. history .......... 53

Chapter 10: Events and Festivals ............................... 55

- Annual events and festivals to experience in North Dakota ................................................................... 56

- Concerts, parades, and cultural celebrations ........... 59

Chapter 11: Off-the-Beaten Path ............................... 61

- Hidden gems and lesser-known attractions in North Dakota ................................................................ 62

- Unique experiences off the tourist trail .................... 65

Chapter 12: Local Tips and Recommendations ......... 67

- Insider tips for traveling in North Dakota ................. 69

- Recommended accommodations, restaurants, and activities ................................................................ 73

Chapter 13: Traveling on a Budget ............................ 75

- Ways to save money while exploring North Dakota .. 76

- Budget-friendly accommodations, transportation options, and dining tips ........................................... 79

Chapter 14: Sustainable Travel in North Dakota ......... 81

- How to travel responsibly and sustainably in North Dakota ................................................................... 82

- Eco-friendly accommodations, tours, and activities 85

Chapter 15: Conclusion ............................................. 87

- Recap of the best places and things to do in North Dakota ................................................................... 88

- Final thoughts on North Dakota as a top travel destination in the U.S. ........................................... 91

# Chapter 1: Introduction

# - Brief overview of North Dakota and its attractions

North Dakota is a state that often gets overlooked, but it is filled with hidden gems just waiting to be discovered. From the rugged Badlands to the rolling prairies, North Dakota offers a unique mix of natural beauty and vibrant culture

One of the most iconic attractions in North Dakota is Theodore Roosevelt National Park. Named after the 26th President of the United States, this park is home to a diverse array of wildlife, including bison, elk, and prairie dogs. Visitors can explore the park's many hiking trails, camp under the stars, or simply take in the stunning views of the colorful badlands.

In addition to its natural beauty, North Dakota also boasts a rich history. The state is home to several Native American tribes, and visitors can learn about their traditions and customs at places like the Knife River Indian Villages National Historic Site. Another must-see for history buffs is

Fort Abraham Lincoln State Park, which is home to the On-A-Slant Indian Village and the reconstructed military post where General Custer was stationed.

North Dakota is also a great destination for outdoor enthusiasts. The state's many lakes and rivers offer ample opportunities for fishing, kayaking, and boating, while its wide-open prairies are perfect for hiking and birdwatching. The Maah Daah Hey Trail, in particular, is a 144-mile-long route that winds through the Badlands, offering incredible views and challenging terrain for mountain bikers and hikers alike.

For those interested in the arts and culture, North Dakota has much to offer as well. The state's vibrant Native American community and rich Scandinavian heritage are celebrated through events and museums like the Scandinavian Heritage Park in Minot and the Plains Art Museum in Fargo.

In conclusion, North Dakota is a state full of surprises and hidden treasures. Whether you're a nature lover, history buff, or culture enthusiast, there is something for everyone in this underrated gem of a state. So, make sure to add North Dakota to your travel bucket list and start uncovering all that it has to offer.

# - Why North Dakota is a unique travel destination

North Dakota is a unique travel destination for a variety of reasons. From its rich history and diverse culture to its stunning natural landscapes, there is much to explore and discover in this often-overlooked state.

One of the most striking aspects of North Dakota is its abundance of natural beauty. From the rolling prairies of the Red River Valley to the rugged badlands of the west, there is something for everyone to appreciate and enjoy. Visitors to the state can take in the breathtaking scenery of Theodore Roosevelt National Park, explore the shores of Lake Sakakawea, or wander through the serene wilderness of the Pembina Gorge. The state's outdoor recreational opportunities, such as fishing, hiking, and birdwatching, are limitless.

In addition to its natural beauty, North Dakota also boasts a rich and diverse history. The state is home to numerous historic sites, including the Knife River Indian Villages National Historic Site, where visitors can learn about the lives and customs of the Northern Plains Native Americans. The state also played a pivotal role in the Lewis and Clark Expedition, and visitors can retrace the explorers' footsteps along the Lewis and Clark National Historic Trail.

North Dakota is also a destination for those interested in arts and culture. The state is home to a vibrant arts scene, with numerous galleries, museums, and theaters showcasing the work of local and regional artists. The Plains Art Museum in Fargo, for example, is a must-visit for those interested in contemporary art, while the North Dakota Heritage Center & State Museum in Bismarck offers a comprehensive look at the state's history and culture.

Overall, North Dakota offers a unique travel experience for those looking to explore a diverse range of natural, historical, and cultural attractions. Whether you are interested in outdoor adventures, learning about the state's rich history, or immersing yourself in its vibrant arts scene, North Dakota has something to offer every kind of traveler. So, if you're looking for a destination that is off the beaten path and full of hidden gems, North Dakota should definitely be on your radar.

# Chapter 2: History of North Dakota

## - Overview of the state's history and how it has shaped its current attractions

North Dakota's rich history has played a significant role in shaping the state's current attractions. The region's indigenous peoples, including the Mandan, Hidatsa, and Arikara tribes, have lived in the area for thousands of years, leaving behind a legacy of culture and tradition that continues to influence North Dakota's modern-day landscape. European fur traders and early explorers also left their mark on the state, further shaping its development.

One of the most notable events in North Dakota's history was the arrival of the railroad in the late 19th century. This brought with it an influx of settlers and led to the establishment of towns and cities across the state. The agricultural and mining industries also flourished during this time, providing the foundation for North Dakota's economy.

This history is evident in the attractions that draw visitors to North Dakota today. The state's numerous historic sites and museums provide a window into its past, allowing visitors to explore the legacy of the indigenous peoples, early settlers, and pioneering industries. From the preserved frontier town of Medora to the interactive exhibits at the North Dakota Heritage Center & State Museum, there are countless opportunities to delve into the state's history.

In addition to its historical attractions, North Dakota also boasts stunning natural landscapes that have been shaped by its past. The Badlands, with their rugged terrain and unique rock formations, offer a glimpse into North Dakota's prehistoric past. The heritage of the indigenous peoples is also evident in the state's cultural attractions, such as the annual United Tribes International Powwow, which showcases traditional dance, music, and crafts.

North Dakota's history has undeniably influenced its current attractions, creating a diverse and compelling tapestry of experiences for visitors. Whether you're interested in delving into the past, exploring the great outdoors, or celebrating the state's cultural heritage, North Dakota has something to offer everyone. With its rich history and hidden gems, the state is a treasure trove waiting to be discovered.

# Chapter 3: Natural Attractions

# - Exploring the beauty of North Dakota's national and state parks

. North Dakota is home to a variety of stunning national and state parks that offer visitors an opportunity to explore the beauty of the state's natural landscapes and wildlife. From the striking Badlands of Theodore Roosevelt National Park to the serene forests and lakes of Lake Sakakawea State Park, there is something for everyone to discover in North Dakota.

Theodore Roosevelt National Park is a must-see destination for anyone visiting North Dakota. This park is comprised of three separate units, each offering unique opportunities to explore the park's diverse terrain and wildlife. The North Unit features expansive grasslands and deep canyons, while the South Unit boasts the dramatic Badlands and scenic overlooks. The Elkhorn Ranch Unit, the site of President Theodore Roosevelt's personal ranch, provides a glimpse into the rugged solitude that inspired one of the nation's great conservation leaders.

Visitors to Theodore Roosevelt National Park can enjoy a wide range of activities, including hiking, wildlife viewing, and photography. The park is home to a variety of animal species, including bison, elk, and mule deer, making it a popular spot for both nature enthusiasts and wildlife photographers. The stunning sunsets over the Badlands make for a perfect ending to a day of exploration in the park.

Lake Sakakawea State Park is another breathtaking destination in North Dakota. This park is located on the shores of Lake Sakakawea, one of the largest man-made reservoirs in the United States. The park offers a wealth of outdoor opportunities, including boating, fishing, and camping. The surrounding area features rolling prairies and wooded valleys, providing a picturesque backdrop for outdoor adventures.

Exploring the beauty of North Dakota's national and state parks is a rewarding experience for anyone seeking to connect with nature and discover the state's hidden gems. Whether you're interested in hiking through the rugged Badlands of Theodore Roosevelt National Park or enjoying a peaceful day on the shores of Lake Sakakawea, North Dakota's parks offer something for everyone to enjoy.

## - Outdoor activities such as hiking, fishing, and wildlife spotting

North Dakota is a state truly blessed with an abundance of natural beauty, and there's no shortage of outdoor activities to enjoy throughout the state. Whether you're an avid hiker, a dedicated angler, or simply someone who revels in the opportunity to observe wildlife in its natural habitat, North Dakota has something to offer everyone.

For those who love to explore on foot, there are countless hiking trails to be found in the many state parks and national wildlife refuges that dot the landscape. Amongst the most popular is the Maah Daah Hey Trail, a 144-mile path that winds its way through the rugged badlands of the western part of the state. This challenging trail offers breathtaking views, dramatic landscapes, and a chance to encounter the native wildlife that calls this area home. Be sure to keep an eye out for mule deer, bighorn sheep, and even the occasional wild turkey as you make your way along the trail.

If fishing is more your speed, you're in luck – North Dakota boasts some of the best angling opportunities in the Midwest. With over 400 fishing waters to choose from, including lakes, rivers, and reservoirs, there's no shortage of places to cast your line. One standout destination is Lake Sakakawea, a massive reservoir on the Missouri River that's renowned for its excellent walleye and northern pike fishing. Alternatively, try the Little Missouri River for a chance to hook a trophy-sized trout, or head to Devils Lake, known as the "Perch Capital of the World," for a day of non-stop action.

For those who prefer a more leisurely approach to experiencing the outdoors, wildlife spotting could be just the ticket. Throughout the state, you'll find an incredible array of creatures, from majestic eagles soaring overhead to adorable prairie dogs peeking out from their burrows. The Theodore Roosevelt National Park, in particular, is home to a diverse array of wildlife, including bison, elk, and wild horses. Keep your camera at the ready for a chance to capture these incredible creatures in their natural habitat.

No matter what your outdoor interests may be, North Dakota is sure to have something that will capture your imagination. So why not lace up your hiking boots, grab your fishing gear, or pack your binoculars, and set out to discover the hidden gems that this remarkable state has to offer? You won't be disappointed.

## Chapter 4: Cultural Attractions

# - Discovering North Dakota's rich Native American heritage

Discovering North Dakota's rich Native American heritage is a fascinating journey through the state's history. The Native American people have had a profound and enduring impact on the culture, land, and ways of life in North Dakota. From their earliest presence to their contemporary communities, North Dakota's Native American heritage is integral to the state's identity.

The origin of North Dakota's Native American heritage dates back thousands of years, with evidence of early human occupation dating as far back as 13,000 years ago. The first inhabitants of the region were the Paleo-Indians, followed by several distinct indigenous cultures, including the Archaic, Woodland, and Plains Indian cultures. Each of these groups made unique contributions to the region's cultural legacy, leaving behind a rich tapestry of artifacts, traditions, and knowledge.

One of the most prominent Native American tribes in North Dakota is the Sioux, consisting of the Lakota, Dakota, and Nakota peoples. The Sioux have a deep connection to the land and have contributed significantly to North Dakota's heritage. Their traditions, language, and customs continue to resonate throughout the state, shaping its cultural landscape.

North Dakota's Native American heritage is intricately tied to the land itself, with sacred sites, traditional villages, and historical landmarks dotting the landscape. It is essential to recognize and preserve these sites, as they provide a vital link to the past and an opportunity to learn from and engage with Native American history and culture.

In addition to the tangible evidence of Native American heritage, the state is also home to vibrant contemporary Native American communities. These communities continue to uphold and celebrate their rich traditions while also adapting to the modern world. Powwows, traditional arts and crafts, and storytelling are just a few examples of how these communities share their heritage with others.

In conclusion, North Dakota's Native American heritage is a treasure trove of history, tradition, and knowledge. Understanding and appreciating this heritage is crucial for anyone seeking to explore the state's cultural richness. With its deep roots in the land and its ongoing presence in modern society, North Dakota's Native American heritage is a vital part of the state's identity, and a source of pride for its people.

## - Visiting museums, art galleries, and historical sites

North Dakota may not be the first place that comes to mind when you think of museums, art galleries, and historical sites, but this hidden gem of a state is actually home to a wealth of cultural treasures. From world-class museums to fascinating historical sites, North Dakota offers a wealth of opportunities for visitors to explore and discover the rich heritage and history of the state.

One of the most popular destinations for history enthusiasts is the North Dakota Heritage Center & State Museum in Bismarck. This state-of-the-art museum offers a comprehensive look at the history of North Dakota, from the days of the dinosaurs to the present day. With exhibits on everything from Native American culture to the settlement of the prairies, this museum provides a fascinating glimpse into the state's past.

For art lovers, the Plains Art Museum in Fargo is a must-visit. Housed in a historic warehouse building, this museum is home to a diverse collection of contemporary and traditional art, including works by regional and national artists. The museum also hosts a variety of art classes, workshops, and special events, making it a popular destination for art enthusiasts of all ages.

In addition to museums and art galleries, North Dakota also boasts a number of historical sites that are worth exploring. Fort Union Trading Post National Historic Site, located near the confluence of the Missouri and Yellowstone rivers, offers a glimpse of what life was like at a 19th-century trading post. Visitors can explore the reconstructed fort, interact with living history interpreters, and learn about the fur trade that once flourished in this area.

Another must-see historical site is the Knife River Indian Villages National Historic Site. This site preserves the remains of the Northern Plains Indian culture, including the Hidatsa, Mandan, and Arikara tribes. Visitors can explore the earthlodge village and learn about the traditional lifeways of these tribes, gaining insight into the rich and complex history of the indigenous peoples of the region.

Overall, North Dakota offers a wealth of opportunities for visitors to explore the state's cultural heritage. Whether you're interested in history, art, or Native American culture, there's something for everyone to discover in this hidden gem of a state. With world-class museums, fascinating historical sites, and unique cultural experiences, North Dakota is a destination that is sure to leave a lasting impression.

## Chapter 5: Adventure Tourism

*- Thrilling experiences such as zip-lining, rock climbing, and water sports*

Chapter 5: Thrilling Experiences in North Dakota

If you're seeking an adrenaline rush or want to test your physical limits, North Dakota offers a wide range of thrilling outdoor activities that are sure to get your heart racing. From zip-lining through lush forests to rock climbing on rugged cliffs, and engaging in a variety of water sports on pristine lakes and rivers, there's no shortage of exciting experiences waiting for those who seek adventure. In this chapter, we'll take a closer look at some of North Dakota's most exhilarating activities and the best places to partake in them.

Zip-lining: Soar through the Treetops

Zip-lining is an exhilarating way to experience North Dakota's beautiful natural landscapes from a unique perspective. One of the best places to partake in this thrilling activity is at the Maah Daah

Hey Trail in the Badlands. Here, you'll find zip-line courses that traverse lush forests, offering breathtaking views of the rugged Badlands terrain below. You'll zip through the treetops, feeling the rush of adrenaline as you fly across the canopy and take in the awe-inspiring scenery. Whether you're a first-time zip-liner or an experienced adventure seeker, the Badlands provide an unforgettable backdrop for an unforgettable zip-lining experience.

Rock Climbing: Conquer the Cliff Faces

For those who love the challenge of rock climbing, North Dakota offers a variety of awe-inspiring cliff faces to conquer. The Dakota Sandstone cliffs in the Turtle Mountains are an ideal location for rock climbing, with their unique formations and breathtaking views. These cliffs provide climbers with an opportunity to test their skills and nerve as they scale their way to the top. Novices can take advantage of guiding services and lessons offered in the area, while experienced climbers can push themselves on these natural rock surfaces.

Water Sports: Enjoy the Rush of Rapids

With its numerous lakes, rivers, and reservoirs, North Dakota is a haven for water sports enthusiasts. Whether you're into whitewater rafting, kayaking, or paddleboarding, there are plenty of options to keep your adrenaline pumping. The Upper Missouri River offers exciting whitewater rafting experiences, with Class III and IV rapids that provide the ultimate thrill for rafters. Additionally, lakes such as Devils Lake and Sakakawea are ideal for kayaking and paddleboarding, offering calm waters perfect for leisurely exploration or more challenging routes for thrill-seeking adventurers.

In conclusion, North Dakota is a treasure trove of thrilling outdoor experiences waiting to be discovered. Whether you're soaring through the treetops on a zip-line, conquering the natural rock formations, or navigating the rushing waters of the state's beautiful lakes and rivers, there's no shortage of adventure to be found in this hidden gem of the northern plains. So, gear up and get ready to uncover the thrilling secrets that North Dakota has to offer.

# - Exploring North Dakota's unique landscapes through adventure tours

Exploring North Dakota's unique landscapes through adventure tours

North Dakota is often overlooked when it comes to providing outdoor adventure opportunities in the American Midwest. However, the state boasts an array of breathtaking natural landscapes, from rugged badlands to rolling prairies. Many of these diverse environments can be actively explored through adventure tours, offering visitors the chance to experience North Dakota's hidden gems in entirely new ways.

One of the most notable natural features of North Dakota is the Badlands. This rugged terrain, carved by millions of years of erosion, offers a unique and awe-inspiring landscape that is perfect for adventurous exploration. Visitors can join guided tours that take them through the Badlands, providing opportunities to hike, rock climb, and even experience the terrain on horseback. As they navigate through the various canyons and cliffs, participants can discover the secret corners of this stunning natural wonderland.

Another iconic feature of North Dakota is its expansive prairies. These vast grasslands are home to a multitude of animal and plant species, making them the perfect destination for nature lovers. Adventure tours in the prairies allow visitors to explore the unique flora and fauna of the area, as well as engage in activities such as birdwatching and wildlife tracking. Additionally, some tours offer opportunities to experience a traditional prairie lifestyle, including activities like bison safaris and cowboy campfire cooking, giving participants an authentic taste of the region's heritage.

North Dakota is also home to a number of serene and picturesque waterways, including the Missouri River and Devil's Lake. Adventure tours centered around these bodies of water provide visitors with opportunities for kayaking, canoeing, and even paddleboarding. The rivers and lakes of North Dakota offer a tranquil and peaceful escape from the hustle and bustle of everyday life, allowing participants to unwind and connect with nature in a truly unique way.

For those with a taste for the extraordinary, North Dakota also offers adventure tours focused on more unusual landscapes. The state is home to a number of unique geological formations, such as the mysterious chasms known as potholes, which were formed during the last Ice Age. Adventure tours exploring these geological marvels provide visitors with the chance to delve into the ancient history of North Dakota and uncover the hidden secrets of its natural environment.

Whether it's hiking through the Badlands, kayaking on the Missouri River, or exploring the ancient potholes, adventure tours in North Dakota provide a unique perspective on the state's diverse landscapes. With opportunities for hiking, wildlife spotting, and immersive cultural experiences, these tours offer an adventurous and educational experience for all who seek to discover North Dakota's hidden gems firsthand. So, next time you find yourself in the Midwest, consider embarking on an adventure tour of North Dakota and uncover its unique and breathtaking scenery.

## Chapter 6: Culinary Experiences

# - Local cuisine and dining options in North Dakota

When visiting North Dakota, travelers can expect to encounter a variety of local cuisine and dining options that truly represent the state's unique cultural and historical heritage. From hearty Midwestern dishes to traditional Native American fare, the dining scene in North Dakota offers something for every palate. Here are some of the top local cuisine and dining options to explore in this hidden gem of a state.

One of the most iconic foods associated with North Dakota is the beloved hotdish. This comforting casserole typically consists of a protein such as ground beef or chicken, mixed with vegetables, and bound together with a creamy soup and topped with a crispy layer of tater tots or buttery cracker crumbs. It's a staple at potlucks and family gatherings, and many proud North Dakotans have their own beloved hotdish recipe that has been passed down through generations.

Another North Dakota favorite is the Bison Burger. As the state animal, bison features prominently in the local cuisine, and many restaurants offer this lean, flavorful meat as an alternative to traditional beef. Bison burgers are often served with unique toppings such as huckleberry jam or cheddar cheese made from North Dakota's own dairy farms.

For those looking to experience traditional Native American cuisine, the local dining scene offers a range of options that showcase the flavors and techniques that have been passed down through generations. Many restaurants serve dishes such as fry bread, a delicious and versatile bread that can be topped with sweet or savory ingredients, as well as other Indigenous-inspired dishes like Wojapi, a sweet berry sauce often used as a dessert or topping for fry bread.

In addition to these local specialties, North Dakota also offers a diverse array of dining experiences that cater to all tastes and preferences. Visitors can find everything from upscale farm-to-table eateries serving locally sourced ingredients to cozy diners and cafes that offer homestyle cooking and classic comfort foods.

Finally, no visit to North Dakota would be complete without trying some of the delicious homemade desserts that the state is known for. From fruity rhubarb pies to creamy lefse, a traditional Scandinavian flatbread, the dessert options in North Dakota are as diverse as they are delicious.

In conclusion, the local cuisine and dining options in North Dakota are a true reflection of the state's rich cultural heritage and agricultural abundance. Whether you're craving a comforting hotdish, curious to try Indigenous-inspired dishes, or simply want to indulge in some homemade desserts, North Dakota's dining scene has something for everyone. So, be sure to explore the culinary treasures of this hidden gem of a state during your next visit.

# - Farmers markets, food festivals, and wineries to visit

When exploring North Dakota, be sure to visit the state's thriving farmers markets, food festivals, and wineries. These attractions offer a rich tapestry of flavors, history, and culture that truly showcase the unique heritage of the region.

Farmers markets can be found throughout North Dakota, offering a charming and diverse array of local produce, meats, cheeses, and artisanal goods. Whether you're strolling through the bustling stalls in Fargo or meandering through the quaint market in Bismarck, the farmers markets are a treasure trove of fresh, seasonal delights. Many vendors are happy to share the stories behind their products, creating a rich connection between visitors and the local community.

For those interested in delving deeper into North Dakota's culinary scene, don't miss the numerous food festivals held across the state. From the Høstfest in Minot, celebrating the Scandinavian heritage of the region, to the Norsk Hostfest in Fargo, these festivals offer a unique opportunity to indulge in traditional and international cuisine while also enjoying live entertainment, cultural exhibits, and arts and crafts.

Wine enthusiasts will find a pleasant surprise in North Dakota's burgeoning wine industry. The state's wineries are producing high-quality wines made from cold-hardy grape varieties, perfectly suited to North Dakota's climate. Visitors can tour the vineyards and sample a variety of wines, from robust reds to crisp whites, all while taking in the beautiful scenery of the rolling hills and valleys.

Notable wineries to visit include the Red Trail Vineyard in Buffalo, a family-owned estate renowned for its superb wines and stunning views, and Pointe of View Winery in Burlington, which offers delicious wines and a charming, rustic atmosphere. Whether you're a connoisseur or simply enjoy a good glass of wine, a visit to North Dakota's wineries is a delightful experience not to be missed.

Overall, farmers markets, food festivals, and wineries are just a few of the many hidden gems waiting to be discovered in North Dakota. These attractions provide an authentic and immersive experience into the state's agricultural and culinary traditions, offering a memorable journey for visitors of all ages. So be sure to make time to explore these captivating destinations and uncover the rich tapestry of flavors, history, and culture that North Dakota has to offer.

## Chapter 7: Small Town Charm

## - Exploring the quaint towns and communities of North Dakota

North Dakota is known for its vast open spaces and stunning natural landscapes, but one of the state's hidden gems is its quaint and charming small towns and communities. These towns offer visitors a unique glimpse into the history and culture of North Dakota, with their well-preserved main streets, historic buildings, and welcoming local residents.

One such town is Medora, located in the scenic Badlands region of western North Dakota. This charming town is steeped in history and offers a variety of cultural and outdoor activities for visitors to enjoy. The town is home to the historic Medora Musical, an outdoor musical production held in the Burning Hills Amphitheatre during the summer months. The musical celebrates the life and times of Theodore Roosevelt, who had a significant impact on the region during his time in North Dakota. Visitors can also explore the nearby Theodore Roosevelt National Park, which offers stunning vistas, hiking trails, and opportunities for wildlife viewing.

Another must-visit town is Rugby, known as the geographical center of North America. This small town is home to the unique Geographical Center of North America monument, which marks the exact center of the continent. Visitors can also explore the Prairie Village Museum, which features a collection of historic buildings and artifacts that provide insight into the region's early settlers and Native American heritage.

In western North Dakota, the town of Hettinger offers a glimpse into the state's agricultural heritage. The small town is surrounded by rolling hills and vast prairies, making it an ideal destination for outdoor enthusiasts. Visitors can explore the nearby Cannonball River, which provides opportunities for fishing, paddling, and wildlife viewing. The town is also home to the Hettinger County Historical Society Museum, which showcases the area's history through exhibits and artifacts.

Heading to the eastern part of the state, the town of Fargo offers a mix of history, culture, and urban amenities. Visitors can explore the historic downtown district, which features well-preserved brick buildings, local shops, and a variety of dining options. The city is also home to several museums and cultural institutions, including the Plains Art Museum and the Fargo Air Museum.

These are just a few examples of the many quaint towns and communities waiting to be explored in North Dakota. Whether you're interested in history, outdoor recreation, or simply experiencing small-town charm, the state's hidden gems offer a treasure trove of experiences for visitors to discover.

## - Meeting locals and experiencing small town hospitality

One of the most rewarding aspects of traveling through North Dakota is the opportunity to meet locals and experience the hospitality of small towns. From the moment you arrive, you can feel the warmth and genuine friendliness of the people who call this beautiful state home.

As you venture off the beaten path and into the smaller communities, you'll have the chance to meet locals who are eager to share their town's history, traditions, and way of life. Whether you're visiting a local diner, striking up a conversation at a rural gas station, or simply wandering through a charming downtown area, you'll find that North Dakotans are proud of their heritage and love to share their stories with visitors.

Small town hospitality is a way of life in North Dakota, and you'll quickly see that the locals are quick to welcome newcomers with open arms. Whether it's a friendly wave from a farmer working their fields or an invitation to join in on a community event, you'll feel like part of the community in no time.

One of the best ways to experience small town hospitality is by staying at a locally-owned bed and breakfast or inn. Not only will you enjoy comfortable accommodations and delicious home-cooked meals, but you'll also have the chance to connect with the owners and learn more about the area from those who know it best. From recommendations for the best local attractions to insider tips on the area's hidden gems, these hosts are always eager to ensure that their guests have a memorable and immersive experience.

In addition to forming connections with the locals, you'll also have the chance to participate in community events and celebrations. Whether it's a small town rodeo, a cultural festival, or a neighborhood block party, these gatherings offer a chance to immerse yourself in local traditions and get a taste of what everyday life is like in North Dakota.

Overall, meeting locals and experiencing small town hospitality is a highlight of any trip to North Dakota. From the welcoming smiles and genuine conversations to the opportunity to truly immerse yourself in the local way of life, these experiences are what make visiting this state truly special. So, don't be afraid to strike up a conversation with a stranger or take a detour to explore a small town – you never know what amazing experiences and connections await.

# Chapter 8: Family-Friendly Attractions

# - Fun activities for the whole family in North Dakota

Looking for some fun activities that the whole family can enjoy in North Dakota? Look no further! North Dakota has a wide range of activities that are perfect for families, whether you're looking for outdoor adventure, cultural experiences, or exciting attractions. Here are some great options for fun activities for the whole family in North Dakota:

Theodore Roosevelt National Park: With its stunning landscapes and abundant wildlife, Theodore Roosevelt National Park is a must-visit destination for families. Take a scenic drive through the park to see the colorful badlands, spot bison and other wildlife, and hike the many trails that wind through the park.

Maah Daah Hey Trail: For families who love outdoor adventures, the Maah Daah Hey Trail is a perfect destination. This 144-mile trail offers hiking, biking, and horseback riding opportunities through the beautiful North Dakota badlands. The trail is divided into segments, so you can choose the length and difficulty level that's right for your family.

Plains Art Museum: If you're looking for a cultural experience, the Plains Art Museum in Fargo is a great option. The museum features a diverse collection of artwork from local and regional artists, as well as traveling exhibits from around the world. It also offers family-friendly programs and events, so you can engage your children with art in a fun and educational way.

Red River Zoo: For a fun and educational outing, visit the Red River Zoo in Fargo. The zoo is home to over 600 animals from around the world, including giraffes, tigers, and prairie dogs. With interactive exhibits, educational programs, and special events, the Red River Zoo is a great place for families to learn about and appreciate wildlife.

Gateway to Science: Located in Bismarck, Gateway to Science is a hands-on science center that's perfect for families with curious kids. The museum features interactive exhibits, live science demonstrations, and a planetarium, offering hours of fun and learning for visitors of all ages.

Maize in North Dakota: During the fall season, families can enjoy a fun and unique activity by exploring one of North Dakota's many corn mazes. These giant mazes are perfect for a day of outdoor fun, with challenges, games, and other activities for the whole family to enjoy.

Always be sure to check the hours of operation and any COVID-19 restrictions before you visit any of these attractions, but these activities should give any family plenty of options to have a great time in North Dakota.

# - Zoos, amusement parks, and family-friendly museums

North Dakota may not be the first place that comes to mind when thinking about zoos, amusement parks, and family-friendly museums, but this state has some hidden gems that are well worth exploring. From the fascinating creatures at the zoos to the fun and engaging exhibits at amusement parks and museums, there's something for everyone to enjoy. So, let's discover the best of what North Dakota has to offer in terms of family-friendly attractions.

Zoos in North Dakota offer a unique opportunity to get up close and personal with a variety of fascinating animals. One standout attraction is the Chahinkapa Zoo in Wahpeton, which is home to over 200 animals, including tigers, monkeys, and more. Visitors can also enjoy attractions such as the Endangered Species Carousel and the playground area. The Dakota Zoo in Bismarck is another must-visit animal park, boasting a diverse collection of species and offering educational opportunities for visitors of all ages.

In addition to zoos, North Dakota also offers a number of amusement parks that are perfect for family fun. One of the most popular destinations is the Red River Valley Fair in West Fargo, featuring thrilling rides, food vendors, and entertaining shows that are sure to keep the whole family entertained. Similarly, the North Dakota State Fair in Minot offers a wide range of exciting rides, games, and live entertainment, making it a perfect destination for a fun-filled day out with the family.

For those looking for a more educational experience, North Dakota is also home to several family-friendly museums that offer engaging and interactive exhibits. The North Dakota Heritage Center & State Museum in Bismarck is a must-visit, showcasing the history and culture of the state through a variety of displays and artifacts. Visitors can explore exhibits about Native American history, early settlers, and even dinosaurs. Another great museum is the Fargo Air Museum, which features an incredible collection of aircraft and aviation artifacts, providing a unique learning experience for all ages.

These are just a few examples of the many family-friendly attractions that can be found in North Dakota. Whether you're interested in exploring the animal kingdom at a zoo, enjoying the thrills of an amusement park, or learning something new at a museum, North Dakota has something for everyone. So, next time you're planning a family vacation, consider adding these hidden gems to your itinerary for an unforgettable experience.

## Chapter 9: Historic Sites

# - Visiting historical landmarks and monuments in North Dakota

Visiting historical landmarks and monuments in North Dakota is a fascinating and enriching experience. The state is home to a diverse range of historical sites that offer insight into the region's rich cultural heritage and storied past. From ancient Native American villages to military forts and iconic monuments, there is no shortage of landmarks to explore in North Dakota.

One of the most notable historical sites in the state is the Knife River Indian Villages National Historic Site. This significant cultural and historical site preserves the remnants of three Native American villages that date back over 600 years. Visitors to the site can explore the earth lodge ruins and learn about the daily lives and traditions of the Mandan and Hidatsa people who once inhabited the villages. The site also features a visitor center with exhibits and interpretive displays that provide a deeper understanding of the area's history.

Another must-visit historical landmark in North Dakota is Fort Abraham Lincoln State Park. Located near Mandan, the park is home to the reconstructed military post that served as the headquarters for George Armstrong Custer and the 7th Cavalry during the 1870s. Visitors can tour the fort's buildings, including the Custer House, and learn about the history of the military post and its role in the Plains Indian Wars. The park also offers scenic trails and beautiful views of the surrounding area, making it a great destination for outdoor enthusiasts.

In addition to these sites, North Dakota is home to several iconic monuments that offer insight into the state's history and culture. The North Dakota State Capitol in Bismarck is a grand architectural marvel that houses the state's government and is a symbol of North Dakota's growth and progress. The state capitol building is open for tours, allowing visitors to admire its stunning art deco design and learn about its history and significance.

The Peace Garden State, which borders Canada and the United States, is home to the International Peace Garden, a vast botanical garden and memorial that promotes peace and friendship between the two countries. The garden features a stunning array of floral displays and sculptures, as well as a 9/11 Memorial, the

Canadian Legion Peace Chapel, and other monuments dedicated to peace and international cooperation.

Visiting historical landmarks and monuments in North Dakota provides a unique opportunity to connect with the state's history and culture. Whether exploring ancient Native American villages, touring military forts, or admiring iconic monuments, visitors to North Dakota are sure to gain a deeper appreciation for the region's heritage and significance. With so many sites to discover, there is always something new and interesting to learn about in historical North Dakota.

# - Learning about the state's role in U.S. history

In the book Discovering North Dakota: Uncovering Hidden Gems, readers will be treated to a detailed exploration of the state's role in U.S. history. From its early days as a hub for fur trading and exploration to its current position as an important agricultural and energy-producing state, North Dakota has played a significant role in shaping the nation's history.

The book delves into the early history of North Dakota, examining the role of Native American tribes such as the Sioux and the Mandan, who were the original inhabitants of the region. Readers will learn about the impact of European explorers and fur traders, who first arrived in North Dakota in the 18th century, and the subsequent settlement of the area by European immigrants.

The text goes on to explore North Dakota's role in the westward expansion of the United States, including its involvement in the Lewis and Clark expedition and the construction of the transcontinental railroad. The book also covers the state's contributions to agriculture, including its wheat and cattle industries, which have helped to feed the nation for decades.

In addition, Discovering North Dakota: Uncovering Hidden Gems examines the state's participation in major historical events, such as the Dust Bowl and the Great Depression, and its role in the development of the energy industry, particularly the discovery of oil in the Bakken Formation.

Throughout the book, readers will encounter fascinating anecdotes, archival photographs, and in-depth analysis of the state's history, offering a nuanced and comprehensive understanding of North Dakota's place in U.S. history.

Ultimately, Discovering North Dakota: Uncovering Hidden Gems illustrates the significant and often overlooked role that North Dakota has played in shaping the nation's history. This comprehensive exploration will leave readers with a newfound appreciation for the state's rich historical heritage and the impact it has had on the development of the United States.

# Chapter 10: Events and Festivals

# - Annual events and festivals to experience in North Dakota

North Dakota is a state rich in cultural heritage and history, and one way that this is showcased every year is through the many annual events and festivals that take place throughout the state. From celebrations of Native American culture to traditional music festivals, there is something for everyone to experience and enjoy in North Dakota.

One of the major annual events in North Dakota is the United Tribes International Powwow, which takes place in Bismarck every September. This powwow brings together hundreds of Native American dancers, singers, and drum groups from around the world to showcase their traditional dance and music. The event also includes traditional arts and crafts, as well as food and demonstrations of tribal and cultural customs. It is a vibrant and colorful celebration that offers a unique opportunity to experience and learn about Native American culture.

Another popular event in North Dakota is the Medora Musical, which is held in the historic town of Medora in the Theodore Roosevelt National Park. This outdoor musical extravaganza takes place throughout the summer months and features a cast of talented performers who showcase a mix of country, western, and comedy performances. The show takes place in a picturesque outdoor amphitheater and is set against the backdrop of the beautiful Badlands. It is a unique and entertaining experience that is not to be missed.

For those who are interested in music, the Fargo Blues Festival is an annual event that attracts some of the best blues performers from around the country. The festival takes place in Fargo, North Dakota, and features two days of performances by both established and up-and-coming blues artists. In addition to the music, the festival also includes food, drinks, and a souvenir market, making it a fun and lively event for music enthusiasts.

Throughout the year, many towns and communities in North Dakota also hold community festivals and events that showcase local heritage, food, and traditions. For example, the Norsk Høstfest in Minot celebrates Scandinavian heritage with traditional food, crafts, and entertainment, while the German Days in Wishek features German music, dance, and food. These events provide a wonderful opportunity to experience the diverse cultural heritage of North Dakota and to meet and interact with locals.

In addition to these events, North Dakota also hosts numerous traditional county fairs, rodeos, and agricultural festivals that provide insight into the state's heritage and rural way of life. These events often include livestock shows, 4-H exhibits, live music, and carnival rides, making them a fun and family-friendly experience for visitors.

Overall, North Dakota's annual events and festivals offer a diverse range of experiences that showcase the state's rich cultural heritage, traditions, and vibrant community spirit. Whether it's dancing at a powwow, enjoying live music in a scenic setting, or experiencing traditional food and crafts, there's always something unique and exciting to discover in North Dakota. These events provide the perfect opportunity to immerse oneself in the local culture and create lasting memories of a truly unforgettable experience.

# *- Concerts, parades, and cultural celebrations*

North Dakota is home to a rich tradition of concerts, parades, and cultural celebrations that showcase the state's diverse heritage and vibrant community spirit. From traditional powwows and ethnic festivals to modern music concerts and lively parades, there's always something to celebrate in North Dakota. Here are just a few of the top events that locals and visitors alike look forward to each year.

One of the most popular cultural celebrations in North Dakota is the annual United Tribes International Powwow, held in Bismarck. This iconic event brings together over 70 different tribes from across the United States and Canada for a weekend of dancing, singing, drumming, and traditional foods. It's a powerful display of Native American culture and an opportunity for people from all walks of life to come together and connect.

For those who are more interested in modern music, North Dakota also offers a wide range of concerts and music festivals throughout the year. The Fargo Blues Festival, for example, draws in music lovers from all over the region to enjoy performances by some of the top blues artists in the country. In addition, the annual North Dakota State Fair, held in Minot, features a diverse lineup of musical acts ranging from country and rock to hip hop and electronic dance music.

But it's not just music that brings people together in North Dakota- the state also hosts a number of vibrant parades and street festivals that celebrate everything from local heritage to national holidays. In Grand Forks, for example, the Potato Bowl Parade is a beloved tradition that marks the start of the local college football season, while the Pride of Dakota Holiday Showcase in Bismarck is a festive affair featuring over 100 vendors selling North Dakota-made products.

Of course, no discussion of North Dakota's cultural celebrations would be complete without mentioning the state's rich ethnic heritage. From the annual Ukrainian Festival in Dickinson to the German Days celebration in Wishek, there are numerous opportunities to experience the traditions and customs of North Dakota's immigrant communities. Visitors can sample authentic cuisine, watch traditional dances, and browse handicrafts at these unique and lively events.

Overall, North Dakota's concerts, parades, and cultural celebrations offer a wonderful opportunity to connect with the state's history and diverse culture. Whether you're a lover of traditional music and dance or simply enjoy a good street parade, North Dakota has something for everyone to enjoy. So be sure to check out the events calendar when planning your visit to this beautiful state- you're sure to find an exciting celebration to attend.

## Chapter 11: Off-the-Beaten Path

# - Hidden gems and lesser-known attractions in North Dakota

North Dakota is home to an abundance of hidden gems and lesser-known attractions that are waiting to be discovered by travelers and locals alike. From scenic byways to historic sites, there is an array of notable destinations that offer unique experiences off the beaten path.

One such hidden gem is the Sheyenne River Valley Scenic Byway, which stretches for 63 miles through the picturesque valley of the Sheyenne River. The byway offers breathtaking views of rolling hills, lush forests, and vibrant wildflowers, making it a perfect destination for nature enthusiasts and amateur photographers. Along the byway, visitors can also explore the Fort Ransom State Park, one of North Dakota's best-kept secrets, with hiking trails, canoeing, and horseback riding opportunities.

Another hidden gem is the Pembina Gorge, located in the northeastern corner of the state. This stunning natural area is characterized by its dramatic river valleys, towering cliffs, and diverse wildlife. The Pembina Gorge State Recreation Area provides outdoor enthusiasts with a multitude of activities, including hiking, mountain biking, and birdwatching. In the winter months, the area also offers opportunities for cross-country skiing and snowshoeing.

For history buffs, the Chateau de Mores in Medora is a must-see attraction. This historic site preserves the legacy of the Marquis de Mores, a French aristocrat who founded the town of Medora in the 1880s. The chateau, which was built in 1883, offers guided tours that transport visitors back in time to the era of cattle ranching, allowing them to explore the beautifully preserved rooms and learn about the fascinating history of the area.

The International Peace Garden, located on the border between North Dakota and Manitoba, Canada, is another hidden gem that offers a peaceful and serene experience. The garden spans over 2,300 acres and features beautifully manicured gardens, hiking trails, and a massive floral clock. Visitors can explore the various themed gardens, as well as the impressive Peace Chapel, which symbolizes the peaceful relationship between the two neighboring countries.

In addition to these hidden gems, North Dakota is also filled with lesser-known attractions that are worth discovering. From the Bonanzaville Pioneer Village in West Fargo to the Knife River Indian Villages National Historic Site near Stanton, there are numerous off-the-beaten-path destinations that provide insight into the state's rich history and cultural heritage.

Whether you're a nature lover, history enthusiast, or simply someone looking to explore new and undiscovered destinations, North Dakota has a wealth of hidden gems and lesser-known attractions waiting to be explored. By venturing off the main tourist routes, travelers can uncover the diverse and captivating beauty of this often-overlooked state.

## - Unique experiences off the tourist trail

North Dakota is often overlooked as a travel destination, but this Midwestern state is full of unique experiences that most tourists never even knew existed. From natural wonders to cultural gems, there's something for everyone who takes the time to explore off the beaten path. In this section, we'll uncover some of the most intriguing hidden gems that North Dakota has to offer.

One incredible experience off the tourist trail is the International Peace Garden. Located on the border between North Dakota and Manitoba, Canada, this 3.65 square mile garden is a symbol of peace and friendship between the two countries. Visitors can explore the beautifully landscaped gardens, attend concerts and events, and even cross the border without needing a passport. It's a truly unique and peaceful destination that many travelers miss out on.

For those interested in Native American culture, a visit to the Knife River Indian Villages National

Historic Site is a must. This site preserves the historic and cultural heritage of the Northern Plains Indians, specifically the Hidatsa, Mandan, and Arikara tribes. Visitors can explore the earthlodge village, stroll through the interpretive trails, and learn about the traditions and customs of these indigenous peoples. It's a powerful and enlightening experience that offers a deeper understanding of North Dakota's history.

Another hidden gem is the charming town of Madora, home to the Theodore Roosevelt National Park. This park is a hidden gem in itself but the town of Madora allows visitors to experience the Old West in a unique and genuine way. From the nightly Medora Musical in the outdoor amphitheater to the horse-drawn carriage rides through the town, it's a step back in time that can't be missed.

If you're a fan of quirky roadside attractions, North Dakota has plenty to offer. The Enchanted Highway is a 32-mile stretch of road featuring the world's largest scrap metal sculptures. Created by artist Gary Greff, these larger than life works of art include a massive grasshopper, a towering tin family, and a giant pheasant. It's a surreal and unforgettable journey that serves as a testament to one man's artistic vision.

And for a truly unique experience, consider taking a trip to the Pembina Gorge. This remote and rugged area is known for its stunning river valleys, scenic hiking trails, and wildlife viewing opportunities. It's a hidden paradise for outdoor enthusiasts, but it's also where you'll find the mysterious and rarely seen natural phenomenon known as the "Pembina Gorge Spires." These towering limestone formations are a rare and extraordinary sight that few have the privilege of witnessing.

From beautiful gardens to historic sites, from small-town charm to sensational sculptures, North Dakota is filled with hidden gems just waiting to be discovered. By venturing off the tourist trail, travelers can uncover some of the most unique and unforgettable experiences that this underrated state has to offer.

## Chapter 12: Local Tips and Recommendations

# - Insider tips for traveling in North Dakota

If you're planning a trip to North Dakota, there are many insider tips and tricks to make your visit more enjoyable and memorable. From where to eat to what hidden gems to explore, here are some insider tips for traveling in North Dakota.

First off, if you're driving through North Dakota, be sure to take advantage of the scenic byways. North Dakota is home to six scenic byways, each offering stunning views of the state's landscape. Some must-see byways include the Sheyenne River Valley Scenic Byway, which takes you through charming small towns and the Pembina Gorge, and the Turtle Mountain Scenic Byway, which winds through the rugged hills and valleys of the Turtle Mountains.

When it comes to dining in North Dakota, be sure to try the local cuisine. From hearty wild game dishes to Scandinavian specialties, North Dakota is home to a diverse and delicious food scene. Don't miss out on classic favorites like the legendary buffalo burger, Norwegian lefse, and hotdish. And if you're looking to sample some local brews, North Dakota's craft beer scene is on the rise, with several breweries offering unique and tasty beers.

If you're a history buff, be sure to add some of North Dakota's historic sites to your itinerary. Fort Abraham Lincoln State Park, the home of General George Custer, offers insight into the history of the American West, while the Knife River Indian Villages National Historic Site provides a glimpse into the lives of the Native American people who inhabited the area.

For outdoor enthusiasts, North Dakota has plenty to offer. With its wide open spaces and diverse landscapes, the state is a playground for outdoor activities like hiking, fishing, bird watching, and wildlife viewing. The International Peace Garden, located on the border of North Dakota and Manitoba, Canada, is a tranquil and beautiful place to explore, with meticulously maintained gardens and a poignant monument commemorating peace between the two nations.

One of the lesser-known attractions in North Dakota is the Enchanted Highway. This 32-mile stretch of road features the world's largest scrap metal sculptures, created by local artist Gary Greff.

The sculptures are scattered along the highway, and each one is a work of art in its own right. The Enchanted Highway is a unique and quirky roadside attraction that is sure to delight travelers of all ages.

When it comes to accommodations, North Dakota offers a range of options, from cozy bed and breakfasts to luxurious hotels. For a truly unique experience, consider staying in a historic homestead or ranch, where you can immerse yourself in the state's rich pioneer heritage.

Finally, don't forget to pack accordingly for your trip to North Dakota. The state experiences all four seasons, so it's important to dress in layers and be prepared for a variety of weather conditions. Whether you're exploring the Badlands, fishing on one of the state's many lakes, or enjoying a cultural event in one of North Dakota's vibrant cities, being prepared for the weather will ensure that you have a comfortable and enjoyable trip.

In summary, North Dakota is a treasure trove of hidden gems, and with these insider tips, you'll be well-equipped to explore all that the state has to offer. Whether you're a history buff, foodie, outdoor enthusiast, or all of the above, North Dakota has something for everyone. So pack your bags and get ready to discover the hidden gems of the Peace Garden State. Happy traveling!

# - Recommended accommodations, restaurants, and activities

Recommended Accommodations:

When visiting North Dakota, there are several great accommodations to choose from. If you're looking for a quaint and cozy bed and breakfast experience, I highly recommend The Red Door Inn in Grand Forks. This charming inn offers beautifully decorated rooms, delicious homemade breakfast, and a warm and welcoming atmosphere. For those who prefer hotel accommodations, The Hotel Donaldson in Fargo is a great choice. This boutique hotel offers stylish and comfortable rooms, a rooftop bar with stunning views of the city, and an excellent restaurant on-site.

Recommended Restaurants:

For delicious dining options in North Dakota, there are a few standout restaurants that you won't want to miss. To experience the best of North Dakota's culinary scene, be sure to visit Pirogue Grille in Bismarck. This fine dining establishment offers a menu of locally sourced ingredients and beautifully crafted dishes that showcase the flavors of the region. Another must-visit restaurant is BernBaum's in Fargo, known for its delicious bagels, sandwiches, and pastries. With a cozy and inviting atmosphere, this eatery is the perfect spot for a leisurely breakfast or lunch.

Recommended Activities:

North Dakota offers a wide range of activities for every type of traveler. One of the top attractions in the state is the Theodore Roosevelt National Park. This stunning park features rugged badlands, scenic drives, and a variety of hiking trails that offer incredible views of the landscape and abundant wildlife. For a unique and educational experience, consider visiting the North Dakota Heritage Center & State Museum in Bismarck. This museum showcases the history and culture of the state through fascinating exhibits and interactive displays. Finally, don't miss the chance to take a scenic drive along the Sheyenne River Valley National Scenic Byway, a 63-mile route that winds through picturesque countryside, charming small towns, and historic sites.

With these recommendations, you're sure to have an unforgettable and enjoyable trip to North

Dakota, uncovering hidden gems along the way. Happy travels!

## Chapter 13: Traveling on a Budget

## - Ways to save money while exploring North Dakota

Exploring North Dakota can be an exciting and enriching experience, but it can also be quite expensive. However, there are several ways in which you can save money while still getting the most out of your North Dakota adventure. Here are a few tips to help you explore North Dakota on a budget:

1. Plan your trip during the off-season: North Dakota is a beautiful state to visit in all seasons, but traveling during the off-peak times can save you money on accommodations, attractions, and even transportation. Consider visiting during the spring or fall when the weather is still pleasant and the crowds are smaller.

2. Look for budget-friendly accommodations: There are plenty of affordable lodging options in North Dakota, including budget hotels, motels, and guesthouses. Consider staying in smaller towns or cities outside of the main tourist areas to find cheaper and more authentic accommodations.

3. Take advantage of free attractions: North Dakota has many free and inexpensive attractions, such as state parks, historic sites, and museums. Take advantage of these opportunities to learn more about the state's history and natural beauty without breaking the bank.

4. Pack your own meals: Eating out every day can quickly add up, so consider packing your own meals for at least some of your trip. Many attractions have picnic areas where you can enjoy a meal while taking in the scenery.

5. Use coupons and discounts: Many attractions in North Dakota offer discounts for seniors, students, military personnel, and AAA members. Look for coupons and special promotions to save money on admission fees and activities.

6. Travel in a group: If you're traveling with a group, consider renting a car or booking accommodations together to take advantage of group discounts. Additionally, many attractions offer group rates for tours and activities.

7. Take advantage of public transportation: North Dakota has an extensive public transportation system, including buses and shuttles, which can help you get around without the expense of renting a car.

By following these tips, you can explore North Dakota without breaking the bank. Whether you're interested in outdoor adventures, cultural experiences, or historical sites, there are plenty of ways to enjoy the beauty and charm of North Dakota on a budget.

# *- Budget-friendly accommodations, transportation options, and dining tips*

When it comes to budget-friendly accommodations, transportation options, and dining tips in North Dakota, there are plenty of options to choose from that won't break the bank. Whether you're an adventurous traveler looking to explore the great outdoors, a history buff eager to learn about the state's rich heritage, or a foodie in search of local delicacies, there's something for everyone in North Dakota.

Accommodations

For budget-friendly accommodations in North Dakota, consider camping in one of the state's numerous public and private campgrounds. From scenic spots along the Missouri River to sprawling grasslands and prairie landscapes, there are plenty of camping options that won't cost you an arm and a leg. If camping isn't your style, you'll also find a variety of affordable motels, hostels, and bed and breakfasts across the state. Many of these accommodations offer basic amenities and comfortable lodging at reasonable rates.

Transportation Options

When it comes to getting around North Dakota, consider renting a car for the ultimate freedom and flexibility to explore the state at your own pace. With relatively low gas prices and well-maintained roadways, driving in North Dakota is a convenient and cost-effective option for travelers. If you prefer public transportation, there are also bus and shuttle services that connect major cities and towns throughout the state. Additionally, biking and hiking are popular ways to explore the natural beauty of North Dakota, with numerous trails and scenic routes to choose from.

Dining Tips

In North Dakota, dining on a budget doesn't mean sacrificing flavor or quality. Look for local diners, cafes, and family-owned restaurants to experience the state's hearty and diverse culinary scene without breaking the bank. From classic comfort foods like hotdish and lutefisk to authentic Native American and Scandinavian dishes, North Dakota has a rich culinary heritage that is reflected in its dining establishments. You can also find farmers markets and food trucks offering fresh, affordable farm-to-table fare and unique ethnic cuisines.

In addition, consider packing picnic lunches to enjoy in North Dakota's scenic parks and natural areas. Not only is this a budget-friendly option, but it also allows you to soak up the state's stunning landscapes while savoring a meal.

Overall, North Dakota offers a wealth of budget-friendly accommodations, transportation options, and dining tips for travelers looking to make the most of their visit without spending a fortune. By taking advantage of these affordable resources, you can explore this hidden gem of a state while keeping your budget in check.

## Chapter 14: Sustainable Travel in North Dakota

# - How to travel responsibly and sustainably in North Dakota

When traveling to North Dakota, it's important to consider how to travel responsibly and sustainably in order to preserve and protect the natural and cultural heritage of the state. Here are some tips for responsible and sustainable travel in North Dakota:

1. Respect the Environment: North Dakota is known for its beautiful natural landscapes and diverse wildlife. When exploring the state, be sure to follow Leave No Trace principles by staying on designated trails, packing out all trash, and leaving natural and cultural artifacts undisturbed.

2. Support Local Businesses: One of the best ways to travel responsibly and sustainably in North Dakota is to support local businesses and communities. Whether it's staying in local guesthouses, eating at locally owned restaurants, or purchasing souvenirs from local artisans, your support helps to strengthen the local economy and preserve the unique character of the state.

3. Choose Green Accommodation: Look for eco-friendly and sustainable accommodation options when visiting North Dakota. Many hotels, lodges, and guesthouses in the state have implemented green initiatives such as energy and water conservation, recycling programs, and the use of environmentally friendly products.

4. Reduce Your Carbon Footprint: Consider traveling to North Dakota by public transportation, carpooling, or using alternative modes of transportation such as biking or walking when exploring the state. If you do need to drive, be mindful of your vehicle's fuel efficiency and opt for car rental companies that offer hybrid or electric vehicles.

5. Educate Yourself: Learn about the local culture, history, and traditions of North Dakota and engage with the community in a respectful and meaningful way. Participating in cultural experiences, attending local events, and supporting heritage sites helps to promote cultural preservation and appreciation.

6. Foster Wildlife Conservation: North Dakota is home to a diverse range of wildlife, including bison, elk, moose, and migratory birds. When visiting natural areas and wildlife reserves, be sure

to observe animals from a safe distance and avoid feeding or disrupting them in their natural habitat.

7. Contribute to Environmental Conservation: Consider volunteering your time and resources to environmental and conservation projects in North Dakota. There are opportunities to participate in trail maintenance, wildlife monitoring, and habitat restoration initiatives that contribute to the long-term preservation of the state's natural resources.

By traveling responsibly and sustainably in North Dakota, you can make a positive impact on the preservation of the environment, culture, and community of the state, ensuring that future generations can also discover the hidden gems of this unique destination.

## - Eco-friendly accommodations, tours, and activities

Planning a trip to North Dakota? Consider adding eco-friendly accommodations, tours, and activities to your itinerary to make your visit not only enjoyable but also sustainable. From cozy eco-lodges to thrilling outdoor adventures, North Dakota has a lot to offer for the eco-conscious traveler.

When it comes to accommodations, North Dakota boasts eco-friendly lodges and resorts that are committed to sustainability. Many lodgings have implemented energy-efficient practices, waste reduction initiatives, and locally sourced amenities. The state also has a Green Lodging Program that recognizes establishments that follow best practices in energy conservation, waste reduction, and water conservation. By staying at these eco-friendly accommodations, you can reduce your environmental impact while experiencing the best that North Dakota has to offer.

In addition to eco-friendly accommodations, North Dakota also offers a variety of sustainable tours and activities. Take a bike tour through the scenic countryside, go bird watching in one of the state's wildlife refuges, or participate in a guided nature hike to explore the beauty of North Dakota's natural landscapes. For a more immersive eco-friendly experience, consider staying at a working farm or ranch where you can learn about sustainable agriculture practices and even participate in hands-on activities such as organic gardening and animal care.

For the adventurous traveler, North Dakota offers a plethora of outdoor activities that are not only fun but also eco-friendly. From kayaking and canoeing on the state's pristine rivers and lakes to hiking in its serene nature preserves, there are plenty of opportunities to connect with nature and minimize your impact on the environment. Another eco-friendly way to explore North Dakota is by participating in wildlife watching tours, where you can observe endangered species and learn about conservation efforts in the state.

When it comes to eco-friendly accommodations, tours, and activities, North Dakota truly has something for everyone. Whether you're looking for a relaxing getaway or an adrenaline-pumping outdoor adventure, you'll find plenty of sustainable options to choose from. By incorporating eco-friendly practices into your travel plans, you can minimize your carbon footprint while enjoying all that North Dakota has to offer.

## Chapter 15: Conclusion

## - Recap of the best places and things to do in North Dakota

North Dakota is a state of surprising diversity and captivating beauty. From its expansive landscapes to its vibrant history, there is no shortage of incredible places to visit and things to do in the Roughrider State. In this section, we'll take a recap of some of the best places and things to do in North Dakota that you won't want to miss

First on our list is the Theodore Roosevelt National Park, a majestic expanse of rugged terrain that was once home to the 26th President of the United States. Here, visitors can explore miles of trails, marvel at the vibrant colors of the badlands, and even spot herds of bison and wild horses in their natural habitat. The park is a haven for outdoor enthusiasts and nature lovers alike.

Next, we have the charming town of Medora, located at the entrance to the Theodore Roosevelt National Park. This quaint western town is filled with history, culture, and a vibrant arts scene. Visitors can catch a live performance at the historic

Medora Musical, explore the unique shops and galleries along the streets, and take a step back in time at the Chateau de Mores State Historic Site.

For those interested in history, a visit to the North Dakota Heritage Center & State Museum is a must. This state-of-the-art facility offers interactive exhibits and artifacts that showcase the rich and diverse history of North Dakota, from its early Native American inhabitants to the modern-day oil boom.

Just a short drive from the Heritage Center is the State Capitol Building, a magnificent structure that is an architectural marvel in itself. Visitors can take a guided tour to learn about the building's history and unique design, and even take in stunning views of Bismarck from the observation deck.

For outdoor adventure, Lake Sakakawea is a top destination for fishing, boating, and water sports. With over 1,300 miles of shoreline, this massive reservoir offers endless opportunities for recreation and relaxation.

And of course, we can't forget about the enchanting International Peace Garden, a symbol of friendship and goodwill between the United States and Canada. This meticulously manicured garden features over 150,000 flowers, scenic walking paths, and even a peace chapel where visitors can pause for reflection.

These are just a few of the countless places and things to do in North Dakota. Whether you're a nature lover, history buff, or outdoor enthusiast, the Roughrider State has something for everyone. As you uncover hidden gems in North Dakota, you'll be rewarded with unforgettable experiences and memories that will last a lifetime.

## - Final thoughts on North Dakota as a top travel destination in the U.S.

North Dakota may not be the first state that comes to mind when considering travel destinations in the United States, but it definitely should be. This hidden gem of the Midwest boasts a unique blend of natural beauty, rich history, and vibrant culture that make it a top contender for any traveler looking to explore a lesser-known corner of the country.

One of the most striking features of North Dakota is its unparalleled natural beauty. From the dramatic Badlands in the west to the rolling hills and expansive prairies of the east, the state is a treasure trove of stunning landscapes just waiting to be explored. Theodore Roosevelt National Park is a must-see for anyone visiting North Dakota, with its otherworldly rock formations, abundant wildlife, and sweeping vistas. Meanwhile, the tranquil waters of Lake Sakakawea and the rugged terrain of the Maah Daah Hey Trail offer endless opportunities for outdoor enthusiasts to hike, bike, or simply take in the breathtaking surroundings.

In addition to its natural beauty, North Dakota is a gold mine of history and culture. The state is home to several prominent Native American tribes, and visitors can learn about their traditions and way of life through the many museums and cultural sites scattered throughout the region. The Scandinavian Heritage Park in Minot and the North Dakota Heritage Center in Bismarck offer a glimpse into the state's immigrant past, while the historic forts and battlefields provide valuable insight into the area's role in the shaping of the American frontier.

Finally, North Dakota's small towns and welcoming communities are a testament to the state's friendly and down-to-earth atmosphere. Whether it's attending a local festival, browsing through quaint shops and galleries, or savoring a hearty meal at a family-owned restaurant, travelers are sure to feel the warmth and hospitality that permeates this often-overlooked state. Indeed, North Dakota's charm lies in its genuine and unassuming nature, providing a refreshing alternative to the hustle and bustle of more popular tourist destinations.

In conclusion, North Dakota is a top travel destination in the U.S. that is well worth discovering. Its natural beauty, rich history, and welcoming communities make it an ideal place for travelers seeking unique and authentic experiences. In a country crowded with popular tourist spots, North Dakota is a breath of fresh air—an unspoiled and underrated treasure waiting to be explored.

Printed in Great Britain
by Amazon